You Got This

A GUIDE TO DITCHING PERFECT AND SHOWING UP TO YOUR REAL LIFE

Jodi King

WESTBOW
PRESS®
A DIVISION OF THOMAS NELSON
& ZONDERVAN

WestBow Press books may be ordered through booksellers or by contacting:

WestBow Press
A Division of Thomas Nelson & Zondervan
1663 Liberty Drive
Bloomington, IN 47403
www.westbowpress.com
1 (866) 928-1240

Interior Image Credit: David O'Donohue

ISBN: 978-1-9736-9540-0 (sc)
ISBN: 978-1-9736-9542-4 (e)

Library of Congress Control Number: 2020911730

Printed in the United States of America.

WestBow Press rev. date: 08/20/2020

Contents

Intro

I think how we act as kids—innocent and unaware—reveals a lot about who we really are. But as our lives unfold—and roles and responsibilities accumulate—it can be so easy to forget that "kid" part of us even exists.

Can you relate?

For me, it's always been singing. I've been singing into my hairbrush for as long as I can remember. My mom told me that when I was about five, she picked me up from Sunday school and asked my teacher if I was well behaved. The teacher would always reply: "She listens well until we invite the class to stand for worship time … and then Jodi instructs everyone to sit down and listen to her sing." How embarrassing! Honestly, though, not much has changed. Instead of a hairbrush, I get to sing into a real microphone. And it's not just my family members in the audience anymore (which is nice).

Fast forward to today. I now tour the country in a band—Love & The Outcome—with my husband, Chris, and our two boys Milo and Ziggy. But there have been a lot of experiences and detours along the journey that have certainly made me question this calling and passion of mine— and forget my why and purpose that began this path in the first place.

We started married life in separate bands, and hardly ever saw each other. When Chris's drummer quit, I bought a drum and asked him if he wanted to join my band and luckily he said yes! We sold our condo to tour in our Jetta—because we were that crazy about each other and living our dreams together. After slogging it out for five years, we signed a record deal, moved to Nashville, had our first baby boy, eighteen months later had our second baby boy.

Instead of packing it in and getting real jobs, we decided to take them on the road and tour as a family of four in our minibus "White Neptune" (clearly, we outgrew the Jetta, thank goodness!).

We hit the road when our babies were six weeks old. I'll never forget how real it got on our first tour as a family of four. I was backstage nursing Ziggy and trying to get ready for the show, which was scheduled to start in five minutes. I tried to put on my skinny jeans and couldn't get them over my hips. I had this cool outfit planned, but Ziggy pooped all over it and I ended up wearing the t-shirt I slept in the night before. I was falling apart and yelled the most honest prayer I had ever prayed "God, you got this?" That night I got up on stage and even though I was far from polished, I had more purpose and passion than ever before. I let people into my real world and that changed everything. Our mess is our message, and we need to let it show!

When I sing, I can hear the Holy Spirit speak and respond in ways I can't off stage. I feel like a kid without a care in the world—known and rejoiced over by my heavenly Father. And that's exactly what I want to communicate to everyone listening, and to you, right now. What lights you up inside? If you're not sure, I bet if you look back over your childhood, you'll see glimpses of that part of yourself. That person is still there. She might just be buried under a few layers of roles and responsibilities that made her grow up and disregard her passions for other priorities. What would it take to make space for some of those things again? Our passions do not have to be our paycheck, but they do deserve a priority place in our lives. Our happiness deserves a vote. Working for the Lord is not a thing; working with the Lord is … and it should be life-giving, not life-sucking.

This book is a collection of questions and conversations with the Lord that I've journaled down over the past two years on the road.

Whether you read one thought each day or the whole book in one sitting, my prayer is that my journey would free you from trying to have it all together and let Him hold you together.

You got this—because He's got you!

Jodi

The God I Know

SAVED TO SET FREE

When I was young, I prayed a prayer asking Jesus into my heart. I continued to pray that prayer over and over at summer camp, church retreats, and any time I felt like I messed up and needed to be resaved. The God I knew as a child was someone who saved me from my mistakes, and that's as far as the relationship went.

When I got into high school, my relationship with God deepened. I realized that being a Christian wasn't just about following a set of rules and playing it safe. It wasn't about being good enough and earning His love. It's about letting that love motivate us to live full and free lives. God doesn't just want us saved: He wants us set free! He wants us to be able to throw our hands up and our worries down at his feet.

Being able to worship on your worst day is a sign that you trust that God's got it. Smiling in the middle of the struggle tells the world around you that you have an anchor for your soul and peace that passes all understanding.

You aren't just saved—you're set free!

Where is your relationship with God at right now?

GALATIANS 5:1

Christ has set us free to live a free life. So take your stand! Never again let anyone put a harness of slavery on you.

If it was all about religion
What to do, what to say
What to wear on a Sunday
All about perfection
Black and white, wrong or right, never grey
Well, I'd never make it
I'd never be good enough
I try to walk the line, pray that I'd find
Something that I knew was real
Began to realize, the harder I tried
The colder I'd start to feel
Until the moment, the second I met Your love
And then I threw my hands up, worries down
I remember when He showed me how
To break up with my doubt
Once I was lost, but now I'm found
No strings attached when He saved my soul
I want you to know, the God I know
Oh, you gotta know, oh, the God I know
He is more than just a rescue
That's where it starts
Not where it ends, let freedom in
More than just a story, in the sky, wearing white
He's alive, in every moment
And now that I know this love
I'm gonna throw my hands up worries down

He Is with Us

THE LONG ROAD IS NOT
THE WRONG ROAD

Have you ever felt like you chose the wrong road? You heard a still small voice calling you out, but now you're wondering if you got it wrong? You've heard a few nos and you're wondering if you should pack it in and head back to the comfortable place you left behind? We wrote the lyrics to this song from our Jetta, in a moment of feeling forgotten and questioning our calling. After a few years of trying to make it happen and playing for pizza, we didn't have much to show for it, except maxed credit cards and a lot of questions. Looking back now, I see that it was our season of preparation for the promise God had spoken over us.

In the middle of living in the Jetta and being financially strapped, our manager got us a showcase for Word Records—a Christians record label in Nashville, Tennessee. Our band that sounded something like Sting meets-Amy-Grant ended up signing a record deal that day and moving to another country. The dream came true, but it looked so different than we thought it would.

I want you to know that the long road is not the wrong road. There are no wrong roads when we're walking with Him—some are just more winding than others. In the wandering and waiting, your biggest tests can develop your deepest trust. Promises you memorized and knew in your head come to life in your heart when you live them out in real time. Putting feet to your faith isn't easy, but it's the only way to grow.

"Success" looks different to me now than it did when I first started dream chasing. The record label, the songs on the radio, the crowds, those are all bonus blessing, but they're not the goal in and of themselves. "Success" is when we are doing what He has tailor-made us for with or without the world's stamp of approval. His consistency has kept us sane on this crazy wonderful journey.

Whether you are in a "success season" or a waiting season or somewhere in between, keep walking through the doors, keep waiting well, keep relying on Him.

What do you need to trust him with today?

> *PROVERBS 3:5,6* (THE VOICE)
>
> *Place your trust in the Eternal; rely on Him completely; never depend upon your own ideas and inventions.*
>
> *Give Him the credit for everything you accomplish, and He will smooth out and straighten the road that lies ahead.*

We can trust our God, He knows what He's doing
Though it might hurt now, we won't be ruined
Might see there's an ocean in between
But he's holding onto you and me
And He's never gonna leave.
He is with us
He is with us
Always, always

King of My Heart

CRITICISM CAN REFINE YOU OR DEFINE YOU

Have you ever felt misunderstood? Try playing a drum on stage in gold leggings and a fur jacket, and channeling Stevie Nicks. Yeah, looking back I can see why I didn't really fit in. To be fair, that was never my goal. I wanted to be an example to young girls everywhere—the example I never had. The voice to women that reminds them: you can sing, serve God and beat a drum, and it can all be worship.

I originally bought the drum to convince Chris to join my band (and it worked!), but I had no idea what freedom it would unlock in me and others when I played it. What started off as a creative expression quickly became my weapon of worship. The only downer was a girl beating a drum onstage was not the norm in contemporary Christian music, and some people didn't get it and decided not to support our band.

I think it's wise to take a beat and consider if there's any truth to the criticism. God, and your people, will let you know if you need to make any adjustments. But let's not forget that the devil loves to hit us where it counts, and will do anything to make us question our calling. But ultimately, we have a choice to make—are you going to allow criticism refine you or define you?

I'm not going to sugarcoat it: those attacks took me out for a while. I didn't play my drum on stage for almost a year, letting the lies that I was not meant to be here leave me powerless. But sometimes it's not enough to call something a lie: you have to replace it with the truth. I had to preach to myself, "I am created by God with a purpose and a creative power that comes from Him. I will not let these critical voices make me powerless." I almost let people's voices speak louder than God's voice.

When we went to a showcase for our label, I knew it was time to take the drum out of hiding. I wanted our soon to-be-partners to know who I really was and where my power came from. In the end, the reason they signed us was not *despite* the fact that we were different, but *because* of that. Surprise—they loved the fact that I played a drum. It set us apart.

If you don't hear anything else I say, hear this: every girl needs a drum. It may not be a physical drum like mine was—but every girl needs to discover their secret weapon in worship—the thing that unlocks your heart to God's and makes you feel beautifully and uniquely made. And don't let anyone take that away.

Because not everyone is going to "get you," but God does because He created you. So the next time you feel misunderstood, remember—His love understands you.

And bring out your drum.

<u>Are you going to let criticism refine you or define you?</u>

GENESIS 50:20 (THE VOICE)

Even though you intended to harm me, God intended it only for good, and through me, he preserved the lives of countless people, as He is still doing today

You are bigger than any battle I'm facing
You are better than anything I've been chasing
Savior and royalty, the only hope for me
Jesus you are, you are
The King of My Heart

Heart Like You

GOD LOOKS AT THE HEART, NOT THE HIGHLIGHT REEL

Have you ever had success take you off course a little? You land that promotion, get into that relationship, achieve that goal—and then somewhere along the way, you become confident in your own abilities instead of relying on Him? Yeah, it happens so easily if we let it.

I still remember we were on the biggest tour of our life to date, Winter Jam, and for the first time in our lives, we had an arena of people singing our song back to us. It was the thrill of a lifetime! After spending so many years living in our Jetta, barely making it by, having a little success felt good. Our songs were on the radio, and our passion had become our paycheck.

We were living the dream, but we'd lost focus. Instead of going after God's heart and being fulfilled by Him first, I was seeking my dreams. And if I'm being honest—achieving them felt good. So I had to come to a place of redefining success. I quickly realized: God is more concerned with our character development than our career highlights.

So I came back to the Lord's Prayer, the prayer we had prayed throughout all of our wandering and waiting, "Thy kingdom come, thy will be done"—not "MY kingdom come, MY will be done." Is our heart set to building His kingdom or our kingdom? Our worth and value is in being His, not by doing His work. You are what He did, not what you do.

<u>What are. you holding tighter than God?</u>

MATTHEW 6:33 (THE MESSAGE)

Steep your life in God-reality, God-initiative, God-provisions. Don't worry about missing out. You'll find all your everyday human concerns will be met

What could be worth more than you
What do I have I wouldn't lose
When it means you and I, look more alike
That's what I choose.
I give up the world to find my soul
Pour out my life give you control
I just want to be what you want me to be
I just want a heart that's true
A heart like you

Ask

PRAY FROM A PLACE OF FAITH, NOT FEAR

My prayers used to be very controlling. Let me give you an example. They sounded a little something like: "God, if you could just do *this*, and work *this* out, and bless me with *this*, **then**...."

It was very "clean" and "neat," but there was no back and forth. I was good at giving God my opinion and my "nice" asks. Oh, man, was I ever. But I was not asking for His opinion. Nor was I being honest with how I actually was feeling deep down. I was praying from a place of fear, not faith—as if He couldn't actually handle the workings of my asking or the messy feelings I was experiencing.

The issue with these stressed-out prayers is that they didn't involve surrender. I was still holding onto my problems. I was being weighed down by things I wasn't ever intended to carry. Do you relate to that?

I'm over praying neat and tidy prayers, ones that looked nice in my journal but aren't honest. Sometimes we have to tell Him how we really feel to get to a place of trusting Him with it.

That's all part of the conversation. God loves hard questions, and he can handle temper tantrums…if I don't get it out with the Lord, I'll let it out on someone else!

It used to mess me up that God wanted me to bring him my requests even though He already knew the outcome, but now I find comfort in that fact. He goes before us, so he knows the best answer. But we still need to ask…

<u>Do you pray faith prayers or safe prayers?</u>

LUKE 11:13 (THE MESSAGE)

Don't bargain with the Lord, be direct. Tell him what you need.

What's on your heart
What dreams do you hold
When do you start
How do you let go
Our Father knows your deepest hurt
Before you've ever said a word
But still He wants to hear your voice
There is a purpose in our seeking
There is a light beyond this door
We have a promise in our knocking
He wants to give us so much more
If we just ask, ask, ask
If we just ask, ask, ask

Breathing In, Breathing Out

YOUR DREAM DOESN'T HAVE AN EXPIRY DATE.

Confession time: I used to believe that if I didn't land a record deal by twenty-five, my dream would never come true. Have you ever believed something like this? That your dreams have an expiration date—and if they pass—you've missed your one chance at them? It can be confusing when we know God has whispered a promise into our heart, but we don't see any signs that it's going to come to fruition. If you've ever felt like this, you are not alone, my friend!

I've been singing into my hairbrush for as long as I can remember. The first time someone trusted me with a real microphone, I was hired to sing a radio jingle selling comfy couches to the tune of fifty dollars. I always knew I could sing, but finding my true voice would take some time. Singing jingles and backup vocals was helpful for refining my craft, but it wasn't what got me excited. The sparks flew when I sang my own song unto the Lord, communicating a truth that God had communicated to me. I loved stepping into who God created me to be, and letting Him light up the gifts.

Maybe your life is full of responsibilities right now that don't leave a lot of room for following your passions. Maybe it even seems frivolous, like a waste of time, to pursue a dream. I get that—I'm home with my kids and often my energy is zapped and I have nothing left to spend on anything else. But God calls us to a full and fulfilling life. What would your life look like if you carved out a little time for yourself and your passions?

Identify a simple, small step toward your passion today. It will make you brave. Reach out to someone who is doing what you'd like to be doing. Show up to that art class that you've been putting off. Put your pen to paper this evening. The road is untraveled: it's yours to pave.

<u>What small step can you take towards your dream right now?</u>

PETER 5:6 (THE MESSAGE)

So be content with who you are, and don't put on airs. God's strong hand is on you; he'll promote you at the right time. Live carefree before God; he is most careful with you.

Sparks fly and my heart runs over
Breathing in / breathing out
Wide-eyed in a moment of wonder
Breathing in, look what you've found
Breathing in / breathing out

No Mistaking It's You

DO WHAT LIGHTS YOU UP AND IT WILL LIGHT UP THE WORLD

Who we are as kids is so telling as to who God has made us to be and what he's given us to use to build His kingdom. I always loved to perform. My mom used to pick me up from Sunday school and ask the teachers how I'd behaved. They would always answer: "Jodi listens well until we ask the class to stand for worship and she tells everyone to 'sit down and listen to her sing'!" Not much has changed—I'm still that same girl, but I get to sing into a real microphone now!

Ever since I was little, there's been this deep knowing that God is lighting me up and the room around me when I sing. An awareness that what was transpiring was bigger than me.

We all encounter God in different ways, and in my life there is no mistaking His presence whenever I get the chance to worship Him through song. Worshipping is my God-given sweet spot, where my talents and His anointing intersect and I can impact others for his kingdom.

Ever since I discovered this sweet spot, I've never looked back. It's taken different forms depending on my season of life, but singing and worshipping is what I was made for, and I will continue to do it no matter if it's on stage or off stage, in public or private, paid or volunteer. None of those reasons are why I started doing this in the first place. It was all because I found God, found myself, and helped others to meet Him, too.

If you are in an in-between season of not knowing exactly what your God-given sweet spot is, I urge you to look back at what you loved to do as a child. Discover how those activities take form in your adult life. And then release all expectations. Step into the journey of finding your calling with the pure heart of desiring to worship the God who created you. And then simply wait to see the awe and wonder come back into your life.

Have you found your God-given sweet spot?

JOHN 1:12 (THE MESSAGE)

He came to his own people, but they didn't want him. But whoever did want him, who believed he was who he claimed and would what he said, He made to be their true selves, their child-of-God selves.

I'd like a burning bush
Wish I could see You like a firework
But I don't need to
'Cause I've seen the proof
Seen the hearts that you move
When You do what You do
There's no mistaking it's You
There's no mistaking it's You
There's no mistaking

The Story You're Building in Me

OUR AUTHORITY COMES FROM OUR STORY

Before we signed a record deal and became the band Love & The Outcome, we were Jodi & Chris, a husband-and-wife duo pursuing their dreams and looking for our next step. LA is the place people go to make their dreams come true, so we decided to give it a shot. We had been touring Canada for several years and wanted to see how far we could take this dream of ours. We had interest from a mainstream record label and decided we would go for it. We saved up, made a plan, and drove until we saw the Hollywood sign.

Then we received a phone call that changed our life.

It was Chris's dad, Bill, calling with the news you never want to get. Helen, Chris's mom, had stomach cancer and it had taken a turn for the worst. Without hesitation, we flew to her to be by her side, left the Jetta and a year's worth of shows, and flew back to Winnipeg.

Helen went home on our seventh wedding anniversary.

Sometimes there are no words to say. All you can do is sit in your pain. Day by day the light creeps back in and a new part of your story begins. Grief is proof of love.

At this point, we put music down and didn't know if we'd ever pick it up again. We told God that if he still wanted us to do music, He would have to make it abundantly clear.

That's when The Newsboys called.

They asked us if we would go on the road with them on a tour across Canada. It seemed the Lord wasn't done with us yet. God never wastes our pain. Maybe you have walked or are walking through loss right now.

You are not alone. God is near the brokenhearted and He is with you now. We all have a story to tell, full of joy and pain. You will make it through this, and that will give someone else hope they will too.

Have you walked your painful road with the Lord or kept Him out of it?

PSALM 126:5 (THE VOICE)

Those who walk the fields to sow, casting their seed in tears, will one day tread those same long rows, amazed by what's appeared.

These are the things that matter in life
Living in every moment, 'cause you can't stop the time
Tomorrow's gonna be yesterday
And I don't want to miss a thing
This is the story you're building in me

When We Love

GOD IS LOVE—WE ARE THE OUTCOME

When I was in my early twenties, I wanted to be single and pursue my music career with nothing holding me back. I was a woman on a mission.

But then I met a man named Chris, who was hot and loved Jesus …and that was my whole list!

My heart flip-flopped, and what started as a solid friendship became an engagement. I remember being at a worship conference a few months before our wedding and sensing the Holy Spirit tell me that Chris would enable certain dreams to be realized that I wouldn't be able to unlock on my own. I didn't understand or see the whole picture, but it was enough of a word from the Lord that I called Chris from the conference and shared what I had experienced.

Slowly we started playing and writing music together. When I was still pursuing my solo career, my guitar player ended up bailing on me one weekend, so I asked Chris if he'd fill in. You know, just for the weekend. He said yes, and off we went to tour together.

That's how it all began.

We had so much fun that we never wanted to come home. A few years later, when I showcased for Word Records, which would later become our label, I played the set that Chris and I created together, and brought him along to play the guitar parts. They loved it. So much actually that they asked if we'd both be willing to leave our solo gigs behind to become a husband-and-wife duo. It was a no-brainer, the obvious next step in the process God had been preparing us for.

So we officially signed a record deal as the duo, Love & the Outcome. God was definitely laying the foundation for what we would one day do together, but that day was a long way off.

Joining forces felt like being assigned a new mission, like when Saul became Paul and God called him to a whole new life. Finding the right band name that represented our new calling was important to us. We prayed and brainstormed, and decided that we wanted it to be more than a name, more like a movement. "God is love and we are the outcome" was an invitation to our fans to join the movement of spreading God's love far and wide, in their own unique way.

<u>Sometimes our dreams look different from God's plan. But His path is much more fulfilling. Do you trust Him with your dreams?</u>

1 JOHN 4:7,8 (THE VOICE)

My loved ones, let us devote ourselves to loving one another. Love comes straight from God, and everyone who loves is born of God and truly knows God. Anyone who does not love does not know God, because God is love.

Hey, are we listening?
There's someone crying out right now
And yeah, we all know what it feels like
When up is really upside down
Everybody's got their story
The hard days and the long nights
Everybody needs somebody
Now might be the time
When we love, when we love, when we love someone
We're the evidence, the evidence of You
When we love like You love, we can see You move
You're alive in us, when we love someone
When we love someone

Paradise

LIVING THE DREAM

Have you ever felt like you're living your life out of order? Your friends are all graduating college and you don't know what you want to do with your life … everyone else is getting married and you're single—yeah, I know how it feels to be behind where you want to be. Chris and I have never done anything in the "right order." We've always lived life on the edge with God at the center, and that has taken us down some unconventional roads! When all our friends were buying houses and settling down, we were selling our condo to live in our Jetta. When everyone else was having babies, we were signing a record deal and *then* having babies and taking them on tour!

But through it all, in every stage, we felt like we were living the dream and that's all that mattered.

Make the life you want to live, not the life your friends are living. Walking out our dreams and callings looks so different for everyone, but trust me when I say that you are right where you're supposed to be. Lean into the Lord's nudges and pay attention to where He wants to take you. Living life to the full is never boring! But you have to be obedient to *your* life's calling and order of events that the Lord has given specifically to you—not the one your friend is living out. Or the one your family expects you to live up to. Or the one you have created in your mind that you *should* be experiencing.

Because *your* version of life to the full with God is always worth it.

<u>Will you let him lead you into uncharted territory or are you going to play it safe?</u>

PSALM 16:11 (THE VOICE)

You direct me on the path that leads to a beautiful life

Catch your breath and close your eyes
You and me forever after
Let's let our plans and dreams collide
We are a beautiful disaster
Never thought life could be this way
Even when it's bad it's good
Me with you, in our own paradise
It's paradise

Louder, Closer, Deeper

IF YOU WANT DEEP RELATIONSHIP, YOU HAVE TO GO THROUGH DEEP WATERS

Have you ever lost the thing you were known for? Maybe it's your job or career path or relationship status. For me, it was losing my voice. We had just played the final show of an arena tour, and although it was the dream come true, I was worn out from the hustle. My voice was completely gone, and I felt like my heart was broken in the process. I remember breaking down on the floor of the airport on our way to Sweden and not being able to get back up.

Ever felt that way? Like you have nothing left to give? I went to see a vocal specialist and he put me on vocal rest for six months. The very thing I had prayed and asked God for my whole life seemed to have been taken away.

It was one of the worst moments of my life, or at least it felt that way. Have you ever felt that? That when you lost something in your life, your identity and purpose were taken along with it?

I remember being in church that Sunday and wrestling through the worship time as I cried my eyes out, begging God to take me out of the situation. What I heard back was not what I wanted to hear, but what I needed to hear. *I won't take you out of your situation—I'll take you through.* That trial built trust between me and the Lord.

When I start to doubt His reliability, I remember back to that season, a time that used to draw me closer and deeper than ever before. Deep calls to deep … if you want deep relationship, you have to be willing to go through deep waters.

Sometimes we can be doing the thing we were made for, but in an unhealthy way. God needed to teach me how to rely on his strength and not my own. He needed to remind me that the voice I'd been given was a gift from Him, not something I possessed. I am worth everything to Him, even if I never sang another note.

You are not your job or your status or your looks. You are valued because you are His.

<u>Will you trust God to walk with you through your situation?</u>

PSALM 42:7 (THE MESSAGE)

When my soul is in the dumps I rehearse everything
I know of you

All my accolades to not define me,
Standing on a stage doesn't qualify me
You're my first call when life hits hard
You're my portions when I've nothing.
If I lose my voice I will only hear Yours speak louder, louder
Lose it all I will only find You are closer, closer.
Death to life, tears to laughter,
You work all things to take me deeper.
So glad I lost myself,
Cuz it's where you found me.
All my shadow days,
You've put behind me.
From my failures you brought freedom,
From my sickness you brought healing.
Speak louder
Draw Closer
Come and take me deeper

What a Promise

MAKE A MIRACLE LIST

I'm a fairly results-driven girl—I like to get things done. Anyone else out there?! But sometimes my greatest strength can become my greatest weakness.

One morning, a couple days before my due date with my first son, Milo, I was freaking out because we were about to release a baby and a record in the same week.

That's way too much releasing, and I was stressed.

So I do what I always do when I'm frantic: I made a "to do" list to tackle before all the releasing began. I thought to myself, *If I can just get all of this stuff done before the baby comes, maybe I'll feel less overwhelmed.* But underneath my coping mechanisms was a girl who was scared to mix two callings: motherhood and artistry. I didn't know what it was going to look like or if I could handle the pressure of it all, so I was trying to control the uncontrollable in the best way my flesh nature knew how.

The Holy Spirit so gently whispered, "Why don't you rip up that 'to do' list and make a miracle list?" A miracle list?! God needed to reveal more to me about this. A miracle list is a list of all the things that I was stressing about that God took care of, the answered prayers and unexplainable peace that I experienced, the provision that only He could bring. It was like He was saying, *Stop depending on what you can do in your own strength and start depending on what I can do through your dependence on me and my strength.* The script was flipped for me that morning. I was no longer burdened by the "make it happen" mentality I had previously lived by, I felt excited for all the ways God was going to work miracles in our life and the lives of others as we walked by faith and not by sight.

God is always doing miracles: we just need to be paying more attention to what he's doing and join in. Now at the end of everyday on tour as a family, we praise the Lord for all the miracles we experienced big and small.

Will you rip up your to-do list and make a miracle list?

PSALM 31:15 (THE PASSION TRANSLATION)

My life, my every moment, my destiny—it's all in your hands.

The sky is dark as we can see it tonight
But You command and the stars defeat it
With Your light, with Your light
We hold the only promise that stays
Won't come and go like today
You are faithful always, always
You will never leave, You will never leave, no
You will never let, You will never let go
If You're what our hope is, then we'll never lose it
What a promise, what a promise, oh
Nothing we can do, nothing we can say, no
Can ever take away, ever take away Your love
You give strength to the faithful
To rise up on eagles' wings
What a promise, what a promise, oh
If the God who spoke my heart into existence
Told me not to worry what tomorrow brings
We'll believe it till we're standing in eternity

Good Life

I HAVE TO VS. I GET TO

Our perspective changes everything, doesn't it? We can view almost anything as a chore or as a joy depending on the way we approach it. For me, cleaning the house is a chore unless I put on my favorite worship playlist and praise the Lord for my boys as I pick up their socks and toys scattered all over the house! My narrative turns from "I have to" to "I get to."

Everything in life is a gift, and remembering that helps us live gratefully not grumpily—even when there are diaper changes involved.

<u>Are you approaching life with an "I get to" attitude?</u>

PSALM 16:9 (THE VOICE)

This is a good life—my heart is glad, my soul is full of joy, and my body is at rest. Who could want for more

Lost here in this moment
Feels like the sky is glowing
Do you ever smile and you don't know why you're smiling?
Days like these are only once in a lifetime
I could just stay here
It doesn't get any better than this
It doesn't get any better
This is a good life!

Galaxies

OUR PLANNING CAN PREVENT HIS PROVISION

God loves to provide for us. He's been where we haven't been yet, so he knows what we need.

He has provision and works from a place of complete knowing. He has gone ahead of, and is preparing us for, what's to come.

Sometimes when I'm impatient, I start to overplan. I like to do things for myself—so I rush ahead and cause myself stress trying to get what I want in an instant, when all along God was going to give me the right gift at the right time. That planning can prevent His provision.

Here's a silly example (that of course meant the world to me at the time).

We had just moved into our apartment in Nashville and, for the first time ever, we had a spare room for family to stay when they came into town. I was ecstatic; compared to the Jetta, this place was a palace! I had my eye on this charcoal-blue Ikea pull-out couch. It was more money than we had to spend, but I had a credit card. As I was justifying my purchase and punching in my details, I felt the Holy Spirit say, *Why don't you wait*. I was annoyed, but I knew it was Him, so I listened.

A few weeks later, right before my parents came to visit, our friends texted and said, "Hey, we are moving to Portland and we have this Ikea pull-out couch that we can't fit in the moving van—any chance you guys might want it"?

I laughed out loud as I read the text! God is so good! He wanted to give me that gift (in the right color I might add), and I almost didn't let Him surprise me.

God doesn't just provide for our needs, He also loves to surprise us with our wants as well.

<u>Will you let Him provide for you today?</u>

ISAIAH 40:28 (THE MESSAGE)

God doesn't come and go, God lasts.

*Why is it so easy to forget
That everything I have all I possess
Is nothing but a gift? You love to give
All You're asking me to do is rest
Your ways are far beyond my ways
Your thoughts are far beyond my thoughts
And still You say I'm always on Your mind
Your words turn into galaxies
Your love is holding gravity
And still you say I'm always on Your mind
What makes me feel the need to run ahead
And miss what's waiting for me in this moment
To be with You is never wasted time
Hear Your whisper, feel Your hands in mine*

Imperfect

HE PERFECTLY LOVES YOU IMPERFECT

I don't have it all together, do you? If your answer is no, then good! Let me be here to remind you that the pressure to prove and people-please is off. God doesn't need you dressed up and trendy—He's cool with messy and imperfect. The only time He can't help you is when you're pretending you don't need His help. Trust me, I know this game. I reach for my red lipstick and leather jacket to look like I've got it all together before I admit to the Lord that I'm falling apart.

Let's spend less energy trying to be something we're not and embrace who we are.

You may break, but you are not broken. You might fall, but you're not a failure. Even when you don't deserve it, He perfectly loves you imperfect.

<u>Are you trying to people-please or letting others see your imperfections?</u>

Psalm 37:5,6 (The Message)

Open up before God, keep nothing back; he'll do whatever needs to be done; He'll validate your life ... and stamp you with approval.

Not all dressed up not all trendy
Not pretending my life ain't messy
Complicated free to show it
'Cause I know you already know it
When I'm making the same mistakes
I know you'll never turn away
Can't lose it can't earn it
You perfectly love me imperfect

Moving On

WHEN WE FEEL STUCK, HE'S STILL MOVING

Have you ever felt stuck? Like no matter how hard you try to move forward, you're standing still? Yeah, me too, and it's one of my least favorite places to be. I recently experienced this feeling when our label was bought and sold and we were stuck in the middle of it all, unable to release music or do what we felt called to do. The whole reason we had moved to Nashville was to pursue the doors God had opened for us music-wise, so this was a very confusing and frustrating season.

My prayers resembled something like, "God you know I hate standing still. I want to go after all the dreams and plans in my heart and I don't want to be in this place anymore." The Holy Spirit kindly whispered back, *I know you like to move forward, but I want you to move your gaze upward to gain my perspective on your situation. You are not stuck; you are on pause for new revelation that will carry you into this new season.*

Wow. The feeling of stuck was gone, and I felt like I was moving even though I was standing still.

Being stuck is a mindset. We can't always control our situation, but we can control our focus in the midst of it. God never sees the problem we see; He sees the promise over our life, and even when you're at a stand still, He is still working.

<u>If you feel stuck, ask God for His perspective on your situation.</u>

ISAIAH 55:8 (THE MESSAGE)

I don't think the way you think. The way you work isn't the way I work.

I've spent my last days standing here
In the shadows of my shame and fear
Where the yesterdays don't disappear
I've spent my last days standing here
I've waved goodbye to my regrets
To the too far gone and can't forgets
Set my sights on what's ahead
I've waved goodbye to my regrets
I, I'm moving on
Guilt has had its grip on me for way to long
This will be my freedom song
Hallelujah because of you I'm moving on
Your second chances never end
I know I will fall down again
Remind me Lord when I forget
Your second chances never end

Falling into Place

WHEN IT FEELS LIKE IT'S ALL FALLING APART, MAYBE IT'S FALLING INTO PLACE

Are you having one of those days where you just need to cry it out? When you believe God is good but life isn't good right now?

I have learned that nothing good comes from holding back my feelings from God and processing apart from Him. God is always up to something good, but to believe, we have to know Him and know His nature.

Making our pursuit of Him and His presence a daily habit and priority creates a closeness and trust that we can rely on in the middle of our hardest days. We can hate our circumstance, but trust God in it.

Don't hold it in; let Him hold you through it. Your faith through the fire will be a testimony to others of who God is to you. Every moment, every tear, nothing goes to waste. God is always up to something good.

He will move the puzzle pieces of your life into the right place at the right time.

<u>Can you trust Him through your tears?</u>

PSALM 34:5 (THE MESSAGE)

Never hide your feelings from Him.

Hold me closer than You ever have
Show me I'm still walking with You hand in hand
Every moment every tear nothing goes to waste
When it feels like it's all falling apart
Maybe it's falling into place

Face to Face

MARRIAGE IS A MIRROR

The first fight Chris and I had as a married couple was over the gym! It sounds hilarious to me now, but I thought everyone was a morning person and wanted to jump out of bed and get after life! Turns out my way is not the only way—my husband gets a vote. Ha!

I've become better at apologizing and accepting Chris for who he is and embracing the ways we are different. We learned a lot about each other in those first few years of marriage—good thing we didn't add being a band into the mix until several years later when the foundation was more firmly in place.

But what this situation showed me is that you can share a life with someone and still not let your guard down. If you're not intentional, you can remain close to your personal desires rather than close to the relationship. If you're not married yet, trust me when I say being married is a mirror, that it helps you see who you really are. Even when it's hard to admit it. But you have to be willing to look and come face-to-face with them and face-to-face with yourself.

And just in the same, God wants to be face-to-face, heart-to-heart with us. He wants us to be close enough to hear His whisper. A whisper is a secret shared between close friends, not passing acquaintances.

<u>Are you intimately connected to the Father? Can you hear His whispers?</u>

PSALM 81:5 (THE MESSAGE)

I hear the most gentle whisper from the one I never guessed would speak to me.

We're standing face-to-face
But why doesn't it feel like we are miles away?
I'm lying in your arms
But why does it feel like we're so far apart?
Our hearts tied together
Times will get better
I'm in this forever, forever, forever

Always Home

LIFE ON THE EDGE
WITH GOD AT THE CENTER

We have become very skilled at making almost anywhere feel like home. It's amazing what a candle can do to make a green room or a hotel room feel cozy.

Home has looked very different for Chris and me over the years. Our first apartment was the cutest little one bedroom in an old downtown building, with a fireplace that worked once upon a time. Character for days, but not a lot of space. We moved into a condo down the street a few years later, and then sold it, and everything in it, to make my first album. Then came the Jetta days, living show to show, making just enough to put gas in the tank.

We upgraded to a fifteen-passenger van that next became our home—and we lovingly named her Jo. That was a luxury at the time. I remember my first tour as a mom, trying to nurse Milo in the backseat with our band members in the front few rows and quietly praying that I wouldn't have to do this for long. Jo died in our driveway the next morning. God answers prayer!

After Jo, we purchased our first ever home in Nashville. After all the moving we'd done, we had only saved a few sacred things; pictures, heirlooms, my red kitchen aid mixer and Chris' guitars. Other than that, everything had been left behind at one place or another.

In that moment, I realized that it doesn't matter where we live; as long as we're together, with God at the centre, we're always home.

I'm not sure if we'll always live the way we do now, with a home life and a road life, but I hope we never lose the ability to hold the puzzle pieces of our life loosely so that God can rearrange them according to His plans and purposes.

<u>Do you live rooted yet open to where God might want to call you?</u>

JOHN 15:4 (THE MESSAGE)

Live in me. Make your home in me just as I do in you.

Cardboard boxes
Filled with moments
Feels like we just moved in
Now we're moving on
One blink, time flies
Hello, goodbye
Loved everyday we spent
Even though these days are gone
But some things last forever
Clocks turn and seasons change
One thing is still the same
Wherever I go, wherever I go
If I have you, I'm always home
My comfort in the tears
My constant all these years
Wherever I go, wherever I go
If I have you, I'm always
Home
Home

Ends of the Earth

SOMEONE ELSE'S WIN IS NOT YOUR LOSS

People tend to believe in you when you're succeeding. And you have to believe in yourself when you're not. Don't wait for someone's affirmation to dig in where you know God is asking you to. Don't be dissuaded by the fact that other people are already doing what you want to do and seem further ahead. If it's in your heart to do, remember that God put it there and you're going to be restless until you try.

Take this book for example. I waited and waited to finish it even though I knew God was asking me to do it. I was hoping someone would come along and tell me what a good idea it was and push me to the finish line. And because of that thought process, the book almost never came out. This would not have been the end of the world seeing as there are a million inspirational books out there, but it would have been devastating to me and my ability to go where God is calling me to next.

You see, when we plant seeds, God doesn't bring a harvest right away. There's the planting, watering, pulling weeds, turning the soil, and a million little steps that need to happen first. It's not a quick process—there's a lot of preparation before the harvest comes. We have to be willing to put in the practice time if we want to get where God is taking us.

Believe me, I know how hard it is to consistently put in the work when it doesn't seem like there's anything consistent about the path you're on. But keep going. Put your whole heart on the line, go after it with everything you have, working unto the Lord and not unto man.

Keep going.
Even when you want to quit—
Even when nobody else gets it—
Even when the applause has died down—
Even when others are thriving—
Even when there's no payment attached—

Nothing flourishes without the sun and the rain. Fruit doesn't just grow in sunny seasons. Keep sowing in the rainy seasons.

Are you making the most of the season you're in?

PSALM 119:1 (THE MESSAGE)

You are blessed when you stay the course, walking steadily on the path revealed by God.

I'll follow You to the ends off the earth
Don't let go of my hand
I'll follow You to the ends of the earth
Lead me through the wasteland
No I'll never look back (never look back, no)
I'll follow You to the ends of the earth

These Are the Days

WHEN GOD CALLS YOU, HE EQUIPS YOU

I never would have guessed that my dream to become a mom would coincide with my dream to be an artist. I would have never thought that I would be career building and family building at the same time! But when God calls you, He equips you for the road ahead. He is with you, and He's gone before you to give you the provisions you need for the season you're in!

Easier said than done, right? There have been days on the road as a family where Chris and I have exhaled "what a day" with an overwhelmed sigh attached. And then there are days where the phrase has happy exclamation points at the end of it with a celebratory high five!

A lesson I've learned that helps me live in the present and juggle both hats whether I'm home or on the road is letting go of what I can't control. It's a lesson that tour life with toddlers teaches you pretty fast, but I'm sure you can relate to that in your own life.

Being out of control can feel like suffering, but when we let go and let God handle it, we can enjoy the moment we're in and be present.

It's also key to keep your priorities front and center. We can't be all things to all people, but God doesn't ask us to be. Right now, my focus is on my family and my artistry and stewarding those as best as I can.

God loves to provide for us. It's part of his job, not ours. He has perfect vision over our life, He can see the complete picture when we only see the problem we're in. When we build our life on this truth, then we no longer have to be scattered and stressed, missing the moments and wasting our days. The urgent is often not the most important. We need to trust that God will take care of what needs to be taken care of as we live in tune with Him.

<u>What do you need to prioritize to be present in your life?</u>

JAMES 4:10 (THE MESSAGE)

Get down on your knees before the master; its the only way you'll get on your feet.

Wake up wake up
Feel your heart beating
Wake up wake up
Alive and you're breathing
These are the days, these are the days
The days we'll never get back
These are the days, these are the days
These days are all we have

Palaces

YOUR GIFTS ARE NOT FOR YOU

G od didn't give me the gift of singing to get famous but to give Him glory. Our gifts and talents are not for us but to save many souls.

Our palaces are temporary and beauty will fade away. When we stand before God, it's our hearts we will bring. Our accolades and medals for reaching the top won't go with us, but how we stewarded our gifts can have eternal consequences!

What are you building in your life right now? Are you making anything a false idol? Whatever you idolize you fear losing, which is where the suffering comes from. Only our Father is worth idolizing, and we can never lose Him.

Have you ever thought about it like that? Your gifts and talents are not for your fame and fortune, to climb the corporate ladder, or be the best of the best. If that happens, then great—we should grow our gifts and do the most we can with what God has given us. But ultimately, what He has placed inside of you is for others. Its for the humans you come in contact with to encounter Jesus and be saved.

Are you using your gifts in the light of this truth?

2 CORINTHIANS 4:18 (THE MESSAGE)

There's far more here than meets the eye. The things we see now are here today, gone tomorrow. But the things we can't see now will last forever.

Our palaces are temporary
Beauty will fade
But when we stand before You
It's our hearts we will bring

If I Don't Have You

HOW TO HUSTLE HEALTHY

Have you ever been in a season of life where you worked from a place of overload instead of overflow?

Girl, me too.

It's so easy to let the scale tip in the striving direction when you're a go-getter and a goal setter. But I'm sure you can attest to the fact that there is a big difference in the stress level when you're drawing from an empty well.

We wrote this song in a hustle season, and at the end of it I realized how unhealthy I had become. I confessed to the Lord, "I don't want to strive and barely survive anymore. It's so not worth achieving these dreams if I'm burned out and far from you. Teach me how to thrive even in the midst of busyness."

There's only one way to do that: learn how to hustle healthy.

When I want to get after something and I forget to ask God His opinion on my pursuit, I end up working hard—not working smart. That path is tiring and stressful. I have found that God can bring me to the same place, meeting that same goal and fulfilling the same dream, in peace and wholeness, no striving attached. When I work from overflow, I work healthy.

What does that mean? It means our *being* determines our doing. I am known by Him so I don't work for approval but from approval. I am loved by God so I don't need to earn His affection. When I spend time being with my Father, all my doing makes sense. There's an ease, even when it isn't easy, you know?!

Today as you work, stop and take note of the place that you're working from. The good news is it's a quick fix to reroute the path to your goals and dreams, with Christ as the driving force behind every action and not your efforts alone. We burn brightest when we abide in Him.

Are you on a path that you initiated and have to maintain? Or are you following God down a path He initiated and will sustain?

GALATIANS 5:16 (THE MESSAGE)

Live animated and motivated by the Holy Spirit

How can I build Your kingdom if I'm building my own
How can You be my treasure if I'm digging for gold
How can You be my fire if my heart has grown cold
How can You be my future if I've made this my home
How can I How can I
I don't want the world if I don't have You
I don't want it all if it means I lose You
I've tasted and I've seen enough
To know it's You I need
I don't want the world if I don't have You
If I don't have You

Gates

WORSHIP IS MY WEAPON

Do you ever find yourself in a stress spiral, letting your anxiety control the day? It's so easy to let our thoughts run wild and before we know it—we're focused on the negative and giving it the power. The opposite of anxiety is thanksgiving. When I feel my stomach tightening or my fists clenched, I release it to the Lord with thanksgiving and praise instead of trying to control what I'm stressed about. I give Him the glory for what He's already doing on my behalf, and thank him for all He has already done in my life.

God doesn't just want us to win the battle in our minds, but also to advance and take new territory. Worship is the way to breakthrough, not just at church but all the time. Making worship and thanksgiving a lifestyle, remaining in His presence continuously—that's the key to maintaining breakthrough. Things that are stressful outside of his presence are not stressful in His presence.

How do you fight your battles?

PSALM 100:4 (THE VOICE)

Go through His gates, giving thanks; walk through His courts, giving praise. Offer Him your gratitude and praise His holy name.

I'm pressing into You
You are my battle song
I fight a war already won
I will run through the gates
With thanksgiving and praise
Into the place where freedom's found
Where all my fears come crashing down
I will run through the gates

I Need You (On Repeat)

THE MESS IS THE MESSAGE

I used to have a very dialed-in morning routine. And then I had kids! I needed to get a handle on this when we decided to take the boys out on their first tour. Milo was eighteen months and Ziggy was a newborn. I was a total disaster. Nursing, singing, nursing, getting on a plane, pumping on a plane, and trying to nail all the roles I was in: mom, wife, and artist. But instead, I wasn't stewarding anything well and I felt I was failing at all the above.

Have you ever been there: holding yourself to an unfair standard because your season has changed, but you haven't changed how you're doing life? Yeah, that pretty much sums up where I was at too.

So I blabbed my face off through tears to God and begged for his help (aka, prayer). I don't know why it took me falling apart to ask for help ... the whisper I heard back was clear as anything I've ever heard. And I believe this is for you, too: "Your mess is the message."

Don't fake that you have it all together. Let people into your messy moments and show them how much you depend on Him for strength. Ever since I started being vulnerable and real about my season, countless women have said this revelation has helped them give up the mom guilt, too. Praise the Lord! Now, instead of a morning Bible study time with Jesus, I'm focused on His presence, my verse of the day—and all the coffee!

But here's the beautiful thing: God is not limited to a formula and He is always ready to meet with us. In fact, all we need to do is turn our attention and awareness to His presence that is always present with us. My morning prayer is "Holy Spirit, I'm here. What do you have for me today?"

So even on your messy mornings, just *be* with Him and the answers will become clear. He will speak to you in the mess, he will speak through you in your mess.

We're all in this together.

Will you let your mess be your message?

ROMANS 8:5–8 (THE MESSAGE)

Those who think they can do it on their own end up obsessed with measuring their own moral muscle but never get around to exercising it in real life. Focusing on self is the opposite of focusing on God.

Hello
It's five in the morning haven't slept a wink yet
Coffee made, I spilled it, made it again
Tell me when does the craziness ever end?
I don't know how I'm gonna hold it all together
Falling apart and it's not even ten
Tell me when does the craziness ever end?
Oh, the mess is the message I've gotta confess it to let you
know
Oh, imperfectly perfect and I know it's worth it to let it show
The scars and the beautiful
Chaos and colorful
Everything in between
I need You, I need You
Like so bad I need You
I'll say it on repeat on repeat on repeat

Same Page

PRIVATE WORSHIP = PUBLIC POWER

There have been seasons where I feel so in step with Chris, and seasons where we have to fight to stay on the same page. Usually it's due to busyness and two toddlers who take a lot of our time and energy. Sometimes it's something silly—like something he said in passing that rubbed me the wrong way. I try to get over it, realize I can't get over it, and by the time I bring it up to him—he doesn't even remember saying it. And I've been stuck stewing on it for a week—unable to move forward!

My relationship with the Lord is the same way.

If we've been out of step, and then I have to step on stage, it's a very uncomfortable feeling. God can use us regardless, but I have so much more to offer when my public life is the overflow of a healthy, private walk.

Does that make sense?

What we do in private is the key to having power in public. Being a worshipper offstage is what makes leading worship onstage work. The more time I spend communing with the Father, the better I communicate with others.

The more time I spend loving the Father, the better I love others.

<u>Are your priorities represented in your private life?</u>

ROMANS 12:9 (THE MESSAGE)

Love from the center of who you are; don't fake it.

I've been moving so fast
I've been walking sidetracked
Panicked, distracted
It makes me feel like
I'm in over my head
Can't tell right from my left
An ocean of emotion
And I'll admit it
I'm drowning in it
Tired of going my way
I want to hear what You say
I wanna be on the same page, same page
Me and You
Yes I do

Seek and Find

PURSUE THE MIRACLE MAKER OVER THE MIRACLE

Do you ever find yourself looking at someone else's life, thinking, *How do they do it?!*

People say that to us a lot when they're watching us navigate life on the road with two toddlers. But everyone's normal is so different. Everyone's calling is different. Everyone's capacity is different. When the Lord calls us, He equips us to handle the situations that come our way.

In light of that truth, do not let your circumstances intimidate you. I know: easier said than done, right!? The more challenging your day, the more resources the Lord will send your way.

One example I can think of is Milo's first fever. We were playing a string of shows in Northern California, and Milo came down with his first high fever. I had never experienced this before, so at the time it was a really big deal. We advance childcare for our shows, which means we depend on a kind stranger at every venue to look after our children while we sound-check and play the show. Typically, we have teenage girls who love playing with our boys, but this particular day, a sweet lady around my mom's age greeted us at the door. She was a nurse, had raised boys of her own, and very familiar with fevers. She taught me how to bring down a fever naturally, a skill I depend on to this day, and kept Milo in such loving care while I got onstage and played a show.

It brings tears to my eyes just writing this down, because God really does send us angels when we need them. When we faithfully serve in the capacity He's called us to, he takes care of us along the way. He shows us that He can be counted on, and my trust in Him grows every time.

<u>Will you trust that He knows what you need today?</u>

DEUTERONOMY 33:25 (ESV)

As your days, so shall your strength be

I don't have all the answers to your questions why
We're all just dreamers and dancers through
the twists and turns of life
All I can tell you is seek and you will find
Seek and you will find
Seek and you will find

I Live for You

NO LIMITS

What limitations have you attached to yourself that are keeping you from stepping into your next season? I always said, "I'm not a speaker—I just sing." Maybe your narrative is "I'm just a mom—I could never start a business." What limits have you put on yourself?

Over the last few years people started encouraging me to speak more, and I felt the Holy Spirit nudge me to start developing and practicing that skill. It felt foreign at first, but I knew if I didn't start taking small steps, I would never be ready for the big opportunities. It's really hard to put yourself out there when you're in the practicing stages, but we don't learn by studying alone: we have to put it into action. In our insta world, it may feel discouraging to start something someone else is already succeeding at. You follow their feed and your feel like why bother. Why bother?! Because you are worth it and God has called you to it!

When God calls you towards something you've never done before, it doesn't mean you get to skip the preparation. He sees what you're capable of, but He's waiting for you to put in the work so you're ready to go when the time is right. Don't limit what the Lord wants to do in and through your life because you're believing the lie that you're not capable. You may not be ready just yet, but with preparation and consistent steps toward the goal, you *will* get there and you will be ready.

<u>What limitations have you put on yourself?</u>

PHILIPPIANS 4:13 (NKJV)

I can do all things through Christ who strengthens me

People ask me what I do
I live the life I'm given to
And I live my life just where I choose
And where I live is close to You
The world keeps turning
I wonder why
But I'll keep living
Or else I'll die
I live for You
I don't know how long I'll live
But all I've got is what I give
So if you're asking what I do
I live for You

City of God

BE VULNERABLE

D o you live with mom guilt? Like going to grab a coffee or do anything by yourself is selfish? Or when someone asks you how you're doing, you respond for your whole family? It's hard to remember who you are sometimes when you are in the season of taking care of little ones.

I feel you: my guilt came from bringing my kids along to work. Early on, we decided not to bring a nanny out on the road with us. I know that sounds insane, but we needed some private family time in the midst of a public life. We decided to ask a childcare helper at every venue we played to watch our boys while we sound-checked and played the show. It was a bit of a learning curve at first, but it ended up being the perfect fit for us. I was able to be mom all day, and then when I needed to do the other part of my calling, the kids hung out with a sweet childcare helper and played with church nursery toys.

Every once in a while, our childcare helper didn't show up. I remember one particular night on a Christmas tour, it was five minutes till showtime and I prayed, "Holy Spirit, please point me in the direction of a trustworthy person who can watch Milo for the thirty minutes we're on stage." I saw a lady at the church who had been hired to cover the merch table and I walked over. I asked for her help and handed her the baby carrier, and she wore Milo for the entire set. As I was thanking her, very apologetically at the end of the night, she told me that she had been diagnosed as infertile—but as she was holding Milo, God renewed his promise to her that she would in fact become a mom one day.

Our need is someone else's blessing. We are all in this together, and God is never doing the bare minimum. He is in the details of everyone's life. From that moment on, I dropped the mom guilt and never again described touring as a family as dragging my kids along. I no longer believe the lie that I'm putting them through this and taking them along for the ride. They are blessed because of it, we are blessed because of it, and everyone who helps us along the way is blessed as well. God has perfect provision.

<u>What do you need to let go of and let God take hold of?</u>

PHILIPPIANS 4:14

Whatever I have, wherever I am, I can make it through anything in the One who makes me who I am.

We are the city
The city of God
And we can't keep it secret
Your love is the light
We will shine

Atmospheres

CREATE SPACE FOR
THE HOLY SPIRIT

We create atmospheres everywhere we go. When Chris and I get onstage, we can't control all the details of the show, but we can create an atmosphere for the Holy Spirit to move. When you go to work, hang with your friends, go to school or mother at home, you carry an atmosphere with you and create one around you. What tone are you setting?

I've always wanted my kids see their mom worship more than worry and complain. I want to be an example of a woman who lives at peace, not overwhelmed. I want to dance it out instead of living stressed out. I want to talk about everything, not fake it till I make it. It's these little realignments that contribute to a joyful and peaceful house (or bus).

What kind of atmosphere are you creating?

> PROVERBS 31:25 (NIV)
>
> She is clothed with strength and dignity; she can laugh at the days to come.

In this place
We've made a space to meet you here
Have Your way
Come into our atmospheres
We've no distractions
We've no demands
We've only open hands
Come and do what you can, what you can only do
Move like only you can, like only you can do
Heal like only you can, like only you can do
Speak like only you can, I only want your truth

You Got This

HIS STRENGTH IS OUR SUPERPOWER

Have you ever had "one of those days," where nothing really goes your way? Yeah me too, the morning we wrote the song, "You Got This!" We were getting ready to head out the door to our first writing session with six-week-old Ziggy in tow. I tried to put on my favorite skinny jeans and couldn't get them over my hips … Chris made me a coffee and I spilled it all over my white shirt … and then right after I changed, Ziggy had a blowout (you can't make this stuff up—check Instagram)! I thought I was superwoman and that this merging of motherhood and artist would be a breeze for me, but it turned out to be harder than I thought. In my moment of desperation, I yelled the most honest prayer of my life, "God, you got this? 'Cause I'm falling apart!" Chris in the other room heard me yelling and said, "Babe, write it down—that's our song! We need to write that song today!"

So we did.

This song not only turned out to be the theme of our album, but also the theme of our life in this season.

Touring with two toddlers is no joke, and "fake it till you make it" is just too tiring to keep up. So I ditched the act and found a way to live life to the full—even though it's full of challenges; depending on Him. My entire definition of confidence has changed from "I've got this" to "God's got this."

This is a book for every woman who shows up for their life—poop stains and all.

Because when we have the courage to show up, give life our best shot that day, and know our power come from Him—we become everyday rock stars. Because We are all rock stars when we live our calling amidst our messy lives. So stop being so hard on yourself: He only sees you through the eyes of love.

<u>What is stressing you out today that you need to let God handle for you?</u>

PHILIPPIANS 4:13 (THE VOICE)

"I can be content in any and every situation through the Anointed One who is my power and strength"

I don't know the way, but You got this
Give me the faith, that You got this
Even today, You got this
I know that I know, God I know that you Got this!

Acknowledgements

My boys...

Chris, for being you. The steady, faithful friend I've been lucky enough to walk through life with. Thanks for cheering me on and helping me go after all my dreams. (and for being my spell check). Lets always make music together, k? I love you.

Milo & Ziggy, you are the greatest gifts I've ever received. You make my life completely wonderful, I love you and I love being your mama. I learn so much from you both everyday. Touring with you in this season is pure joy, and I hope we always get to do everything together. And...thanks for having long naps at the same time so I could write this book :)

Dad...

For seeing the next step before I do, even when I think you're crazy! For showing me that failure is success when we learn from it and try again. You have given me the tools to never quit.

Mom...

For empowering me to be who I am. For always growing and evolving and encouraging me to do the same. Thanks for showing me what being a mom looks like. You are the best at it.

Dad Rad & Carla...

For always being in my corner and loving us so well...even if it means driving a million miles to pick us up and help us get to our next destination.

My brothers & sisters...

Each of you encourages me to a better human because of how you love and serve others with your gifts. I love you all so much.

My Team...

Andrew, for your wisdom, guidance and friendship. You always help me see the big picture. None of this would be possible without you.

Pat, for being thoughtful, strategic and patient. You helped me bring this book to life.

Elizabeth Evans...

For walking with me through this process and helping me believe in my voice. You were a key part of this process, and I'm so grateful.

Kyla...

For being my sounding board and encouragement

Hillary...

For being my first Nashville friend and always being such a cheerleader in my life

Rod Riley...

For always taking time to meet with me and believing I had something to say. You lead by example, so glad our paths crossed.

Alex Seeley...

For showing me what it looks like to be fearlesly in love with The Father and not reign it in or tame it down. I've become more courageous because of you.

Jordan Lee Dooley...

For workshopping the title with me and making yourself available when I needed your expertise.

Bob Goff...

For seeking vulnerability and honesty in all you do and encouraging me to do the same.

Natalie Grant...

For inspiring me everyday by the way you live your life and sing about it, and having a coffee with a no name girl from Canada.

Ms.Melonie & Sydni...

For being family and making our lives work. I'm so thankful for you both.

Joel, Katie, Caroline & Bennett...

For making home feel like home

Auntie Susan...

For letting us eat all your strawberries

Uncle Harold...

For letting the boys wander over and play in your garage, and for bringing us flowers and making us smile.

Thank you to everyone on this list for partnering with me to make my book dream possible. I am forever grateful for each and every one of you. My prayer is that every time you read these pages you would gain fresh perspective from the Father and that these verses would move from your head to your heart to the foundation you walk on everyday.

Brenda Zabriskie

S. Loewen

Cara Barrows

Julie Ogren

Denise Willerton

Kristjana Hale

Diana L. Quintanilla

Debb Michiels

Murray & Jodeen Aide

Cynthia Milbeck

J Michael Orr

Uncle Joel & Aunt Katie

Keith and Cynthia Bedford

Kim Bonhomme

Kristin Leslie Rosol

Pam and Steve Sutter

Larry Alan Krimmer

Christy Welch

Priscilla Bighetty

William R. Shade

Chelsea Revis

The Zellar Family
Sarah Postma
Lisa Gaska
Pam Watson
Nellie Yager
Raymond and Chanel Gonzales
Victor E. Parr
Taha Boles
Amy R. Zimmerman
Barb Stubbs
Sandy Boosel
Mrs. Marcel Bergansky
Tammie & Jim Downey
Mark Mertens
Savannah Marie Tuss
Ginny Beck
Mike Schnell and Lyn Miller
Nick & Meghan VonMuenster
Louise Hargrave
Stephanie Kobelinski
Mary Cross
Jessica Morgan
Danielle Platek
Victoria Tedder
Brooke Randolph
Jodie Fowler
Skufca Family
Mariann Gaston
Sophia Lujan
Brenda Mendoza

Steve & Kay Hortman
Madelyn Dennis
Moriah Hunter
Samuel Moreno
Nicole Fisher
Ellen Wright
Amy Kling
Christi Sayre
Susan Foley
Angela Gladden
Trish Wilson
Brian & Hope Eber
Bill Rademaker
Irene Gorsky
Steven J Crowell
Elisa
Mrs. Tammy
The Stenner Family - Shane, Hillary, Tobin, Iva, Kit, & Lev
Hope and Healing International
Amanda Hlavaty

About the Author

Hailing from Winnipeg, Manitoba, Jodi King is one half of the husband and wife duo Love & The Outcome. After throwing caution to the wind and selling their condo along with everything in it, touring Canada selling CD's out of the trunk of their Jetta, the couple landed a record deal with Word Entertainment / Warner Music Group in 2012. Their self-titled debut album, *Love & The Outcome*, released the following year to critical acclaim and the duo has since become one of the most compelling emergent voices in the Contemporary Christian music space. Their highly-anticipated sophomore album, *These Are The Days*, released the same week their first baby boy Milo was born. The 'band' was complete eighteen months later when Ziggy entered the world! Instead of packing it in and getting 'real jobs', Jodi and Chris bought a bigger vehicle and took the family on the road. In Jodi's words: "When you're a wife, mom, artist and living your life in public, perfection is impossible… walking with purpose is not. This shift in perspective from 'I've got this' to 'God, I know that you've got this' is what sets this work apart". To date, Love & The Outcome have amassed a loyal, engaged audience, earning over one hundred million streams globally, tens of millions of impressions, achieved multiple Top #5 songs on the Billboard chart and shared stages with their peers including for King & Country, TobyMac, Lecrae and Switchfoot. With 20 GMA Canada Covenant Awards and nominations, Juno Award and KLOVE Fan Award nominations to their name, Jodi and Chris continue to share their music worldwide. Their latest single, "Moving On" impacts Christian radio in June 2020 and their third LP, *You Got This*, is scheduled for release later this year.